Book Description

Is your teen being rebellious? Do they talk back and not obey rules? Are they always hiding stuff from you or lying to your face? Are they being difficult on purpose and seeking complete independence?

Teenagers, with the numerous changes going on, can be challenging to handle. Their sudden need for privacy and independence can drive you nuts. Your once obedient and compassionate child seems to have grown into this monstrous hulk, ready to charge whenever something doesn't go according to their plans.

So how do you handle the temper tantrums, prevent arguments and disagreements, establish some ground rules, and ensure that they follow them? This parenting book has the answer.

Written in a simple and undeviating manner, it equips parents with 7 vital, strategic, effective, and well-researched skills, which, if implemented, will send all their concerns and worries out the door. To give you a quick overview of what to expect, take a look at the many important topics it covers:

- Importance of setting a positive example
- The need for positive attention and spending quality time with them
- Handling teenage anxiety and helping teens overcome it

- Picking up the right battles to fight for
- The best strategies to set realistic expectations for teens
- Purpose of allowing teenagers some room and space to breathe
- The important role effective communication plays

All these topics and many more are discussed in detail to help parents seeking advice and recommendations on what to do and what not to. The 7 vital parenting skills we discussed will definitely help you raise them to become responsible, independent, emotionally-intellectual, and happy adults.

7 Vital Parenting Skills for Understanding Teenagers and Communicating With Teens

Proven Parenting Tips for Developing Healthy Relationships for Teens and Reducing Teen Anxiety

Frank Dixon

professional advice. The content within this book has been derived from various sources. Please consult a licensed professional before attempting any techniques outlined in this book.

By reading this document, the reader agrees that under no circumstances is the author responsible for any losses, direct or indirect, that are incurred as a result of the use of the information contained within this document, including, but not limited to, errors, omissions, or inaccuracies.

Before we begin, I have something special waiting for you. An action-packed 1 page printout with a few quick & easy tips taken from this book that you can start using today to become a better parent right now!

It's my gift to you, free of cost. Think of it as my way of saying thank you to you for purchasing this book.

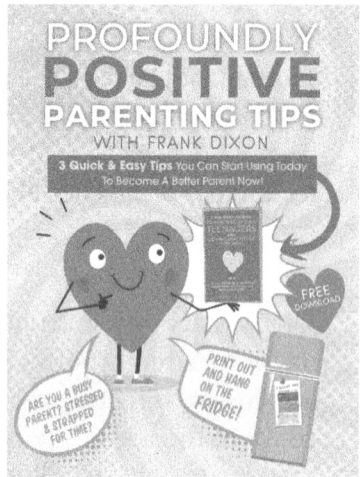

Claim your download of Profoundly Positive Parenting with Frank Dixon by scanning the QR code below and join my mailing list.

Sign up below to grab your free copy, print it out and hang it on the fridge!

Sign Up By Scanning The QR Code With Your Phone's Camera To Be Redirected To A Page To Enter Your Email And Receive INSTANT Access To Your Download

Before we jump in, I'd like to express my gratitude. I know this mustn't be the first book you came across and yet you still decided to give it a read. There are numerous courses and guides you could have picked instead that promise to make you an ideal and well-rounded parent while raising your children to be the best they can be.

But for some reason, mine stood out from the rest and this makes me the happiest person on the planet right now. If you stick with it, I promise this will be a worthwhile read.

In the pages that follow, you're going to learn the best parenting skills so that your child can grow to become the best version of themselves and in doing so experience a meaningful understanding of what it means to be an effective parent.

Notable Quotes About Parenting

*"Children Must Be Taught How To Think,
Not What To Think."*

— Margaret Mead

"It's easier to build strong children than to fix
broken men [or women]."

- Frederick Douglass

"Truly great friends are hard to find, difficult
to leave, and impossible to forget."

— George Randolf

"Nothing in life is to be feared, it is only to be
understood. Now is the time to understand
more, so that we may fear less."

— Scientist Marie Curie

Table of Contents

Introduction

Remember the night your baby kept you awake all night, crying and needing to be fed, and all you could think to yourself was that this will soon pass? Well, now you have the same child, grown up into a teenager and that night of sleeplessness feels like a beautiful dream. You had thought that having lived through the middle-of-the-night feedings, temper tantrums and hectic school routines, you will finally have some years of quiet and calm. Alas, those golden years don't seem to catch up to you any time soon because you now have a rebellious, raging with hormones, disobedient, rude, and ill-mannered child in the house and have no clue how to deal with them.

For many parents, teen years are a rather confusing period. Their kids are showing intense growth, fluctuations in their moods, and emotional instability. But they aren't just difficult, they also have upbeat energy that is hard to compete with, a growing and idealistic mindset, a deep interest in what's right and wrong, and thoughtfulness. They are finding themselves and learning to associate themselves and nurture their talents, skills, and passions.

It is scary yet beautiful.

There is no given timeline as to when adolescence begins. For most girls, it starts around the age of 13 and for boys, much later when they are 14 to 16 years of age. In different parts of the world, the average varies, which means everyone's normal is slightly different. Many of us, for most of our lives, have believed that reaching puberty means the development of sexual characteristics, such as an increase in breast size, onset of pubic hair, and menstrual periods in girls. In boys, the earliest signs of puberty are the growth of their testicles and scrotum. But these are just physical changes. Many emotional and behavioral changes take place too, but since they aren't visible changes, they often get neglected, which is where problems begin to sprout from. The most common behavioral changes happen around their parents. As they seek more independence, they start to separate from their parents. They become more concerned than ever about what others think of them, especially their peers. They try different looks, pursue multiple interests and passions, and try to fit in the world. When they struggle with these, episodes of distress happen. Conflicts with parents also increase. A classic example of this could be a teenage daughter arguing with her mother because she wants to wear something more provocative and edgy than what her mother had selected for her. After all, all her friends are dressing in the same manner. The argument can lead to serious accusations such as, "You want me to make a fool out of myself wearing that", or, "You don't care about what my friends will think of me if I go wearing what you chose for me."

This time of emotional ups and downs has been of great interest to psychologists and scientists for many years. For many years, they have been trying to break through the stereotypical image of what being a teen feels like and want to learn more about what goes on in their heads.

The more knowledge we have, the better parenting skills we can bring into practice to minimize the number of conflicts and disagreements.

Therefore, in this book, we look at how teenagers behave, the many changes they go through, why they seem so stressed and anxious and how, as parents, we can help them navigate through this complicated chapter of their lives with grace. To begin with, we look at various parenting skills, which if applied, can help parents understand their growing children better and help them cope with the challenges they face by offering emotional support. There are many questions we shall look at such as, "Am I giving my child enough room and explore themselves or being a control-freak", or "If I need to allow them more independence to engage in age-appropriate activities or not", or, "If I am being the right role model for them or not."

So let's begin!

Chapter 1: Brain Vs. Hormones

Since most of the changes that take place reflect or have an impact on the way teenagers behave, we must discuss these early on so that we start off on the right foot and ease into the normality of living with a teenager in the latter part of the chapter.

Two prominent changes suggest the onset of maturity in teenagers. The first is bodily changes and the second, emotional. Both are regulated by the hormonal fluctuations in their bodies. They help with the development of the brain as well as the inception of puberty which triggers many bodily changes, suggesting sexual maturity.

Hormonal changes guide the body through puberty and this, for the most part, includes the increase in the levels of testosterone in boys and estrogen in girls. They are responsible for the majority of behavioral changes such as mood swings, aggression, depression, anxiety, and more.

Secondly, the changes in the level of maturity of the brain. New and promising research studies propose that the brain continues to mature well after teenagers turn 18. We now also know that hormonal changes don't trigger the changes in the brain but the brain triggers the hormonal changes. Yet, there is still no certainty of what triggers what, as it is observed that late bloomers or children who don't undergo puberty due to hormonal issues also have a perfectly mature brain working normally. There have been no visible differences in the way they question things, assess risks, or get along with their peers.

Some of the most common changes in the brain during the teenage years include neural messages and neural connections.

Neural messages speed up thanks to the addition of myelin to the neurons. This makes everything get through faster.

Secondly, a large number of neural connections in the prefrontal cortex are pruned which makes things like planning, organization, and implementation of tasks more efficient. This happens during adolescence when the brain takes a time-out, which means, during this specific period, the functioning of the brain is less effective – thus the poor decision-making skills and risk assessment.

These two, when together, the result is some noteworthy behavioral changes most commonly linked with teenagers. For instance:

Limited Functioning of the Brain: The changes in the prefrontal cortex – the region of the brain responsible for regulating logical thinking and its aspects – causes lapses in good judgment and risk assessment. This is what makes them high on energy at all times which results in an enhanced need for risk-taking and life-threatening behavior. Since they aren't thinking straight, they subject themselves to exploration which doesn't always end well for them. Drunk driving and drug overdose, to name a few.

Increased Need for Excitement: Since messages are traveling faster than ever, teenagers experience an increased need for sensory input. It usually manifests itself as adrenaline-seeking. Ever wondered why places like theme parks and clubs target teenagers specifically? It is because they are more likely to respond well to activities that involve some form of risk or excitement.

Heightened Emotional Responses: Teenagers, during adolescence, also feel things more strongly. You may spot them causing a scene out of the blue, crying their eyes out over something trivial, and walk back to their room after slamming the door into your face. There are days when they will be over the moon with joy and happiness and also days when they won't come out of their room for the entire day unless to eat. In girls, such mood swings are more prevalent as they tend to feel things more deeply.

Focus on Self: Let's get one thing straight: teenagers aren't deliberately trying to be rude or selfish. They genuinely have a troubled time deciphering emotions in others, again, due to the rewiring of the prefrontal cortex. This makes them rather self-centered. They don't care about the impact their actions and words have on others.

Goals When Living With a Teenager

Keep in mind, all teenagers are different and unique. Give them some space and time to open up to you and while they do, encourage and appreciate any form of communication they try to have with you. Other than that, there are some ground rules as per an article in Psychology Today that all parents must abide by when they have a teenager in the house.

Learn to Ignore Disobedience

We are all aware of the eye rolls when told to do something uninteresting. It can make your blood boil but you have to control your emotions. If they notice that it irritates you, they will do it more often. Shake it off and don't feel disrespected. Although since it isn't an acceptable way to handle orders, sit them down when they are in a good mood and try to bring it up by telling them how disrespected you feel when they do it.

Change Their Definition for the Word 'Sexy'

If you have a teenage daughter, tell her that sexy doesn't always mean knee-high skirts or crop tops that barely cover anything. Tell her the kind of message she is sending by wearing such revealing clothes. Let her know that if she truly wishes to look sexy, then she should go with what feels comfortable and not with what everyone's wearing. Sexy can also mean intelligence, straightforwardness, and confidence. Their goal shouldn't just be to invite male attention but to make the right statement. It has nothing to do with revealing clothes.

If you are raising a teenage boy, he must know not to give in to peer pressure and get involved in things beyond his age such as alcohol, smoking pot, taking ecstasy pills, or sniffing chalk without proper knowledge of what it can do to their systems. No, it isn't sexy – just self-threatening.

Have the "Talk"

For many parents, it is one of the most dreadful days when they have to sit down with their teenager and go through the details of sex, sexual orientation, and protection. Peggy Orenstein, in her book Girls and Sex, tells her readers that although many girls act tough when demanding equality on the field and in the classroom, they succumb to the pressures of sexual activity due to their partner's wishes. As they are more informed than ever about these things, we need to have a clear and detailed dialogue with them about why they should never settle for anything demeaning to please someone. The same is the case with most teenage boys. Influenced by what their friends are doing or into, they indulge themselves in self-harming or reckless behavior in the name of fun.

Apologize for Bad Behavior

It can be called miraculous if you never fought about anything with your teenager. You must have yelled, shouted, or shamed them for their choices in a weak moment when you felt that things were slipping out of your hand. However, now is the time to teach them a valuable lesson i.e. the power of forgiveness!

If you have thrown your power around, misused it around them or shamed them in one way or the other, own up to it and apologize. An apology requires commitment and sincerity and it is an essential thing to teach your teenager. It requires that the guilty submits to their mistakes without any shame and expects being treated fairly in return. If they model it and begin to admit to their mistakes, they will be more willing to rectify them instead of just giving up or hiding in fear.

Show Patience Towards Their Lack of Empathy

They can be egomaniacs and stubborn. They may not understand your need to have some space to yourself because you are feeling down. They may also seem too involved in their problems and issues. This lack of empathy is normal for a teenager to demonstrate. Don't be too surprised or hurt by how selfish they can be. It is just a phase.

Be Cautious When Discussing Their Friends

They may not like the way you talk about their friends or understand why you don't like them. As their focus changes from family to their friends, they may become sensitive about them. Therefore, whenever approaching the topic of discussing their friends, take caution. If you have a bad feeling about a friend of theirs, don't just say it out loud. Use other strategic ways to make them understand why you think they are a bad influence. For instance, you can concoct a story about how you also had a friend like theirs and how you ended by being hurt because of them.

Act Like a Grown-Up

Remember who the adult is in the house. Make them know it too. This doesn't mean making decisions for them or laying down strict rules and regulations in the house. It means that they know who is in charge of having the last say in the house and why they must do what they are told. Teenagers need us as their role models and moral compasses. You have to be compassionate and considerate but also authoritative. They must know that they can never exploit the privileges they enjoy.

Chapter 2: The 7 Vital Parenting Skills to Understanding Teenagers

Most parents think it is they who deal with the most challenges, but it is only one side of the story. Teenagers are equally clueless about the changes happening inside them. They feel unprepared to cope with them in healthy ways and thus, become more anxious than ever. Teenage anxiety is a real thing and also one of the most worrying types of anxiety. If we look at the statistics in the US alone, approximately 4.4 million children aged 3 to 17 have anxiety. That accounts for an astounding 7.1% of the teenage population. One point nine million of these teens develop symptoms of depression, and need serious help and therapy.

Something is very wrong here and everyone – the media, society and adults are to blame. Since there is not much we can do about the internet or the society that poses high standards and expectations from teenagers, what we can do is help them be prepared for it. Chances are, if they are already past their sixteenth birthday mark, you don't have much time left. They will soon be out, relying on the mercy of others, their knowledge, and academics to help them find their place in the world.

Therefore, we thought about this in detail and wanted to present parents with a collective list of strategies and methods, which if implemented correctly, can help teenagers relieve some of the stress they feel.

In a world that judges us more for our choices and not for our strong character and academics, it has become easier to just pull someone's leg and bring them down. Cyberbullying has been on the rise too. Screenshots and videos of highly-intimate messages are shared all over the internet without the consent of the other involved party and left to be blamed and shamed. Teenagers, influenced by their peers, want to do things they would never approach with a sane mind because why not – if everyone is doing it, it must be okay. Remember the tide-pod challenge? Did you know some of the teenagers stopped breathing and had to be put on a ventilator to stay alive? The point is, kids will always want to try things that entice some level of thrill and excitement. They would want to try things, just for the sake of trying.

So what can we do?

Help them make better choices. Help them take calculated risks. They shouldn't go in blindly or run after things without assessing the associated risks. They should be confident enough to call out the stupid people who put theirs and others' lives at risk just for some likes and comments under their name. They should know when to call it quits before things get out of hand. They must know how to deal with their emotions , no matter how overwhelming they are. They should never lose control over them and know to deal with them in better and healthy ways.

So how can we teach them these?

Vital Parenting Skills

Let's look briefly at each one in action and see how it can help both parents and teenagers to be on the same page, cultivate better communication, and have strong interpersonal relationships.

With our 7 vital parenting skills! What are they? Let's introduce them to you.

Vital Parenting Skill #1 - Setting a Positive Example

First and foremost, teenagers need a parent figure they can look up to. Most of the behaviors children pick up are the ones they observe others around them doing. You must have had those moments where your toddler tried to imitate the way you talk on the phone or how their father washes the car. Therefore, it is essential that whatever they are learning from us is high-quality, healthy, transparent, and rewarding. It is our job to ensure that whatever habits and behaviors they take from us help them grow up to be a better person. Think of it as choosing the best materials to lay the foundation of a building. High-quality cement, sturdy bricks, strong iron rods, etc. If you want it to stay high and tall and be praised by everyone, you need to ensure it can stand on its own.

Vital Parenting Skill #2 - Giving Positive Attention

The second thing they need from you is positive attention. When kids feel valued and looked after, they feel safe and secure. They feel supported and confident. Parents should, therefore, spend quality time with their kids from the start to impart the right values and habits. Family times can mean a lot of things. It can mean doing things of interest together, going on trips together, watching TV, eating dinners, or simply taking the time to talk. Ideally, there should be a weekly ritual where the whole family gets together and shares the top highlights of the week. In chapter four, discussing this in detail, we shall see how positive attention helps teenagers in the longer run.

Vital Parenting Skill #3 - Reducing Teen Anxiety

Another vital skill that parents must have or practice is teaching their children ways to cope with negative emotions such as anger, anxiety, depression, and other mental health conditions in a positive way. They must use means that don't add to their teenager's stress levels and engage them in things that help alleviate it.

Vital Parenting Skill #4 - Picking Battles

Not all battles are worth fighting. Some errors and mistakes are to be ignored and not argued over. There is no point in deliberately trying to create rifts over trivial things, as you don't want your teenager to look at you as a constant nagger. This will ruin the relationship you share with them and they will start to distance themselves from you. They will begin to avoid you when at home and not reply to you when questioned, because they don't want another fight. If you are trying to understand them and make communication better between you two, then you need to be smart about the things that can lead to a heated conversation. You need to understand their need for privacy and not keep losing your temper every time they leave their dirty clothes on the floor instead of putting them in the laundry basket. Instead, you have to find strategic ways to deal with the problems that bother you and in this chapter, we shall look at some in detail.

Vital Parenting Skill #5 - Setting Reasonable Expectations

The next essential skill on the list is reasonable expectations. Many parents, unknowingly, burden their children with more than their weak shoulders can handle. They push them into extra-curricular activities they are not interested in and prevent them from following their passions. There is no harm in wanting to increase the prospects of your teenager leading a successful life by asking them to become an accountant instead of a chef or a musician but science is now proving that kids who choose to follow their dreams are much happier and content with their lives than those who don't. Therefore, as a parent, you have to set the right expectations for them and help them craft a path to live, but it needs to be up to them. You can't just leave them in the dark. You have to help them figure out the things they want from their life and help them achieve them. This is both a skill and a necessity.

Vital Parenting Skill #6 - Make Communications Stronger

Another parenting skill that parents must practice is working on the communication between them and their teenagers. This is, by far, the hardest thing to do, keeping in mind that they have a mind of their own. As parents, you have to ensure that they are not doing things they shouldn't be doing behind your back or keeping secrets that can be self-harming. You have to identify the barriers to communication and work on them to improve it.

Vital Parenting Skill #7 - Giving Them Some Room to Breathe

Finally, parents don't need to act as a disciplinarian or authoritarian. They have to allow their kids some space to explore age-appropriate things. If you are too strict and unforgiving, they may go behind your back and still do the things that you don't want them to do. Instead, you have to let them come to you with their problems without probing them about them too much. You have to let them have some moments to themselves, try to figure out things their way and only intervene when they allow you to.

All these are discussed in the following chapters in much detail with the "whys" and "hows" to help the readers gain a better sense of what goes on in the mind of their teenager and how to understand them better.

Chapter 3: Essential Parenting Skill – Setting a Positive Example

Children are born without social skills or social knowledge. They eagerly wait to find someone they can mimic. That someone is mostly the one closest to them – their parents. You are your child's very first teacher and guide. You teach them how to eat, clean, and sleep. You teach them how to sit straight, walk, jump, or chew a bubble gum without digesting it. Did you know that our kids are more affected by what we allow them to witness than what we tell them? It is interactions and visual evidence that hold more value in their eyes. They might not want to clean their rooms but will eventually learn to do it if they see you cleaning up yours. They might not want to try different foods if they see you sticking to some basics. They will not model good behavior or pick up good habits if you don't practice them. Whatever behaviors they pick up, they pick up from us, which is why it is highly crucial to set the right example.

You have to live by the rules you want them to abide by. You have to lead a life that reflects the values and morals you want to instill in them. You have to walk the talk because if you don't, they won't either. You can't go complaining about how messy they are if you are messy too. You have to be a positive role model they grow up watching. Your goal should be to make them want to be like you, even when they become teenagers.

As parents, we often underestimate the value of healthy habits and behaviors. We don't invest the amount of time or energy needed to mold our children in the best manner possible. We leave them in the hands of the world, their peers, teachers, and even strangers to teach them things. We think if they don't do it now, someday experience will teach them. What if this is where we fail as parents? What if, not being the right role model is the biggest mistake? What if this is the reason why they feel so insecure about themselves, suffer from low self-esteem, and are always stressed?

Thus, it is about time you start thinking about what you are leaving your son or daughter with. Have you made them competent enough to follow their passions and live a successful, brave, and autonomous life?

Lack of a Role Model and Teenagers

In 2019, during one of the largest surveys by the Prince's Trust, it was revealed that 67% of adults who have grown up without a positive figure of the same gender were more likely to be unemployed than those who grew up with one ("Youth Index 2019," 2019). The survey stated that 2.170 people were interviewed between the ages of 16 and 25. The following were some other significant findings that pose the importance of a positive role model in the lives of teenagers.

- One in every 3 men had no positive figure to look up to. One in every 4 women stated the same.
- The lack of a positive role model impacted the mental wellbeing of those affected significantly.
- They had an overall negative outlook on life.
- They had trouble staying employed for longer periods as opposed to their peers.
- They were three times more likely to suffer from mental illnesses like depression and anxiety, and told the interviewers that they didn't recall the last time they felt proud of themselves.
- 50% of the women who grew up without a female positive figure in their lives told that at some point in their lives, they had felt suicidal.
- One in 4 teenagers reported that they lacked a sense of identity.
- One in 5 men said they had turned to illegal drugs and engaged in criminal activities due to the stress of being unemployed.

All these statistics are proof that a positive role model in a teenager's life is pivotal. It can be life-changing for most and save them from ending up in jail or staying unemployed.

And that is not all, in another survey conducted by Barna Group, looking at the need for positive role models for teens, found that the majority of the teenagers had listed their parents as the ideal role models in their lives (Teen Role Models: Who They Are, Why They Matter, 2011). No, it wasn't celebrities or athletes or influencers. Parents were the most highly regarded individuals because they offered moral support, encouragement, and love.

Who Are Role Models?

This is an important question to ask ourselves. Who are role models? Are they just the subject of emulation and admiration? Are they the ones who inspire others to strive for success via their attributes and achievements? Are they the ones who are always present and interact with their children giving them consistent attention?

Well, they are all that and more. Role models are the ones teenagers look up to when searching for their identities. They are the ones who lend an ear to listen, pat us on the shoulder when we do something good, cheer on for us when we feel unconfident, and shelter us from harm.

Being the Super Hero They Need in Their Lives

Being a role model requires forethought, effort, and self-control. It isn't easy to keep your cool when your child misbehaves or pushes your buttons intentionally. But since you have to set the right example, you choose composure and calmness over yelling and punishment. This is a huge responsibility you have on your shoulders and being aware of it can motivate you to do better. For instance, if you don't want your child to learn to yell, you have to stop yelling too. Other than that, you will have to:

Preach by Example

The first thing you need to do is stop being a pretender and walk the talk. With children, "do as I say" doesn't work – at least not in the longer run. They need to observe the consistency in your words and actions. It's simple really.

- If you want them to eat healthily, you eat and cook healthy.
- If you want them to limit the use of technology in the house, you do the same first.
- If you want them to not lie or use it as a means to get away with something, you have to stop lying about being sick and skipping work.

You have to make them appreciate you for being true to the rules you want to preach.

Examine Your Behavior and Reactions

Since they are looking up to you at all times, you must model the right behaviors via your actions and reactions. For example, you must know how to control your stress and anger, how to respond and handle unforeseen problems, how to express your anger and other negative emotions, how to deal with mistakes, responsibilities, competitions, and loss, how to take care of your body and mind, etc. If you are doing well, then you are setting the perfect example for them to follow.

Be Forgiving of Mistakes

No one is perfect. Mistakes are bound to happen. However, what's important is the way the situation is handled. Your teenager needs to see if you are forgiving or accepting when someone makes a mistake. They need to see if you deal calmly when things go wrong or berate the perpetrator. They need to see if you play the victim card and blame others or own up to your mistakes and shortcomings? They need to see you apologize when you are in the wrong, and look for strategies to not do better the next time.

Address Conflicts Sensibly

You have to make them see you deal with your problems in a calm and composed manner. They don't need to see you throwing things at your spouse or the neighbors over a small fight. Because chances are, if later, you go up to their room to preach them about the importance of conflict management, they are going to call you out. They also need to see you manage your goals such as weight loss or eating healthy foods so they learn to stay true to their commitments. Even if you fail, you have to tell them that it is alright so that they don't feel pressured constantly to aim for perfection.

Practice Modesty and Respect Towards Others

Your kids don't only see you, they hear you too. What language you speak, how you approach others, talk to them, or speak about them behind their backs are things that say a lot about your character. They listen to how you talk to your partner, your friends, relatives, neighbors, or strangers at a department store. They notice if you show respect towards them or not. They notice the tone and pitch of your voice. They notice how you practice tolerance when stuck in traffic or when someone bypasses you on the highway. They notice the way you cuss or use abusive language when in a foul mood. They notice how you speak to them and in what tone. They notice if your words are harsh and threatening or compassionate and kind. They notice if you misbehave as a response when angry or if you keep your cool. To set the right example, you have to be cautious of the way you speak around them and the language and tone you use.

Chapter 4: Essential Parenting Skill – Giving Positive Attention

It is natural for parents to want to discipline their teenagers when they misbehave. They point out their faults, yell at them, or try to correct them with punishments. Though it makes sense, this approach to parenting can backfire.

New studies discussed later in the chapter reveal that positive disciplining or attention has proven more effective in changing behavior in the long-run. The simplest way to do so is by praising the behaviors you want them to demonstrate as opposed to calling out the behaviors that you deem to be negative.

But that certainly doesn't mean that parents have to look away every time their teenager misbehaves and only applaud them for the good things they do. Since more clarification is needed, let's begin with what positive attention is and how it can benefit teenagers by improving communication and reducing anxiety.

Positive attention requires that you praise your child for good behavior or a job well done and ignore, at least at the moment, the negative behavior. The goal is to offer parental attention – one of the things teenagers need the most. When we put positive attention into practice, it involves catching your teenager when they are doing something good.

Positive parenting can take many forms. It can include physical contact (hugs, kisses, and pats on the back) or emotional support like verbal and non-verbal praises such as high-fives and rewards. According to Lindsay Gerber, a clinical psychologist at the Child Mind Institute, parents need to be more specific and descriptive. This means that they don't only need to say, "Good job", but rather, "Good job cleaning your room. It looks so clean. I am so proud of you." She believes this increases the likelihood of replication of that behavior.

The Power of Positive Attention

Not only that, but there are also many other studies and research articles that link positive attention with improved behavior, happiness, and satisfaction in adolescents. For instance, one study suggests that positive attention from parents improves psychosocial functioning in teenagers (Joussemet et al., 2008). Another suggests reduced symptoms of depression, and better self-esteem (Duineveld et al., 2017). Another study suggests that positive attention from parents, peers, and educators build social self-efficacy in them (Coleman, 2003).

Spending quality time with children has also reported improvements to their self-esteem. They feel more validated by the emotional support offered to them and feel confident about the relationships in their lives. Another key factor here is that positive parental attention also boosts a child's academic aspirations. They are more confident to follow their passions, dedicate themselves to achieving their goals, and show greater interest in extracurricular activities. Finally, giving your teen positive attention can establish a healthy relationship between you two, which will reduce their behavioral problems and set them up for success.

5 Ways to Give Positive Attention

So what activities or interests can you two sign up for in order to spend some quality time together? How can you take time to appreciate them and celebrate their small victories and good behaviors? Take a look!

Ask Them About Their Day

Teenagers can succumb to the pressures of social media, friendships, and relationships, etc. They need some positivity in their lives and someone to talk to about the worries and stresses they experience. As a parent, you can offer them the moral and emotional support they need. All you have to do is ask them about their day every day, hoping they will open up to you. Asking our children this simple question allows them to see that you care about their wellbeing, worry about their happiness, and wish to offer comfort, in case they need it. When they will feel looked after, valued, and validated, they will be more open and compassionate.

Seek Their Opinion Over Things

They aren't little children anymore. They have had a taste of the outside world which means they are growing up to become sensible. Including them in household decisions such as deciding on a monthly grocery list, seeking their opinion on what they think about the house chores, what should be cooked for dinner, etc. This will make them feel valued and respected. When their input is taken into consideration, they will also feel more confident in expressing themselves with you.

Help Them Follow Their Passions

As a parent, another way you can provide them positive attention is by showing interest in their lives and the goals they wish to achieve. You can sit them down and have a detailed chat about where they want to be and what they want to be doing in the next 10 years.. You can help them map out a plan or map out the steps they need to take to achieve their goals.

Plan a Trip Together

It's another thing to go on one and another to plan one. Both promise equal fun so engage them in both. Spend time together to decide where you should go, what clothes and accessories you should pack along, what places you should visit, etc., etc. If a trip isn't a possibility, for now, you can go on smaller ones over the weekend together. You can go on a hiking trip, boating, to the beach, shopping, or visiting places of interest, etc.

Develop Healthy Habits

These include eating well, exercising, writing a gratitude journal, and sharing your thoughts. As they say, you have to be the role model they need. You have to set the right example if you want them to change. For instance, we all know that regular physical activity alleviates stress by releasing dopamine in our systems, which makes us feel good. They are less likely to listen and obey you when you tell them to exercise, and more likely if you get on board with them too. Besides, you can always keep checking in on them too.

Chapter 5: Essential Parenting Skill - Reducing Teen Anxiety

National Institutes of Health suggests that nearly every 1 in 3 teenagers aged 13 to 18 experiences an anxiety disorder (Any Anxiety Disorder, 2017). According to the Child Mind Institute, 9% of all teenagers suffer from some form of an anxiety disorder (social, GAD, panic, separation, etc.).

In recent years, the statistics are unbelievably bad. If we look at the rates of suicides and suicidal attempts, the picture gets even darker. This leaves many parents with some concerns and worries. Is their child suffering from an anxiety disorder? Are they happy with their lives? Are they happy with us as their parents? Are we doing enough to foster happiness and joy in their lives?

Although feeling anxious is a normal reaction, it becomes problematic when it happens all the time. But why is my teenager stressed? They don't have to worry about putting food on the table, paying the bills, or raising kids. What can be so heart-breaking or scary that they choose to indulge in self-harm activities or try to commit suicide?

Let's discuss some of the most common, yet overlooked reasons that add stress in the lives of our adolescents.

Factors That Contribute to Teen Anxiety in Today's World

If we go back in time and remember when we were adolescents, were we as anxious? Were we that stressed? Was there so much societal pressure to live up to? So how did we get here? Where did we go wrong in raising our kids as independent, happy, and confident adults? Several factors contribute to anxiety and impatience in teenagers today. These include:

Unrealistic Expectations and Pressures to Succeed

We have so many expectations from our children today that they are collapsing under the burdens of it. During a survey, an interviewer asked incoming college freshmen if they felt overwhelmed by the expectations their peers and parents had of them or not. Forty one percent of them said yes in 2016, compared to 28% in 2000 (Eagan et al., 2016). You can do the math. The data has doubled in the last few years. We want them to be good at school, take part in social causes, learn a new language, join karate, play an instrument, be a part of a sports team and what not, without even realizing that we are setting them up for failure.

The World Is Becoming Scarier

We have seen a rapid increase in school shootings, violence, bullying, and lockdowns. People have been exposed to all sorts of crimes on the street and in their homes. The world is no longer a safe place for them to live in. So it is acceptable to feel scared and threatened. They see it every day on their phones, on TVs and thus, feel like they have to be cautious at all times.

Social Media Is Becoming Addictive

Children and adolescents are bullied online. They also feel like they don't have enough. They notice the big things others are doing, what resources they have, how privileged they are, and then they look at their sad and boring lives and become depressed. They feel nothing remarkable will ever happen to them and this lowers their self-esteem. They compare themselves to others and feel like they aren't beautiful, intellectual, or wealthy enough to compete with them, and it further makes them feel like a loser.

Adult Responsibilities Are Making Them Anxious

We have also loaded them with adult responsibilities, knowing very well that their brain is still developing to take on them. They lack the skills they need to finish them and it causes frustrations. They want to go back to the time when things were easier and less complicated. They are fed up with the constant reminder that they need to grow up and act responsibly.

They Lack Healthy Coping Mechanisms

They know little about emotional skills or how to deal with their problems and anxiety. As parents, we emphasize more on their academics than on their emotional health. According to a national survey, the majority of teenagers feel unprepared to start college and live on their own (Morin, 2017). They suffer from separation as well as social anxiety and it is much higher in naturally shy teenagers. They don't have sufficient knowledge or skills to combat stress, take care of themselves, or manage their time.

Exposure to Drugs and Alcohol

Teens crave thrill and excitement. They want to know what it feels like to get high or drunk and thus, often expose themselves to things that are hard to pull them out of. They know they shouldn't indulge in such activities and yet they do, just because there has always been something very exciting about trying the thing that is forbidden. They become addicted, and they will become anxious every time they feel the need for it and not have it around them. They will also exhibit many behavioral problems that will ruin their relationships with others.

Peer Pressure Is Higher Than Ever

Teenagers are also under a lot of pressure from their friends. If they are surrounded by negative or unhealthy friends, they will indulge in activities they aren't supposed to indulge in, just because their friends do. They want to live up to the expectations of them and follow in their footsteps, even when they are taking them in the wrong direction. In the case that your teenager's friends are all getting good grades, excelling at extracurricular activities, and getting scholarships from excellent colleges and your teenager isn't, you can imagine the amount of stress they are in.

How Can You Help?

Management of teenage anxiety is essential. It is an important life skill that you need to teach them. If they feel anxious, panicked, or stressed out, they need to know what to do in all of these situations and prevent it from becoming worse. First of all, you need to tell them that it is a completely normal reaction to have and it will go away in time. You must also tell them that they shouldn't allow it to come in the way of things they need to do and continue without submitting to it. For example, they may have a big class presentation coming up that is causing them to sweat. Sit them down and talk to them about how they don't need to let it get into their heads and mess everything up. You can also teach them some breathing techniques to allow a good flow of oxygen to the brain to keep them calm and composed.

Managing anxiety is an important life skill. As a parent, here's what you need to do:

1. Acknowledge their fears. Don't tell them that they are being foolish and dramatic. If they seem genuinely scared, then you need to take them seriously and help them overcome it. For example, if your teenager is scared of needles and needs to get a flu shot, you need to acknowledge it and help them cope with it.

2. Encourage them to take on the things they are afraid of. However, there is no need to go overboard and force them into doing it. It will only add to their fears.

3. If they want to withdraw from something out of fear or anxiety, let them - without creating a fuss about it. Let them know that it is up to them if they want to quit but do let them know that you have confidence that they will manage it well if they choose to go after it.

4. Appreciate their efforts to overcome stress and anxiety, no matter how small they are. They need to know that they can count on you to be on their side instead of shaming them for being a loser.

5. Have conversations about the time when you were scared of something and then later overcame it. Sit them down and talk to them about the things that helped you overcome

your fears. Stories that inspire and motivate can boost their self-confidence.

6. Keep them nourished with healthy food choices, especially young girls, Encourage the intake of fresh fruits and vegetables in their diet, motivate them to keep their bodies in shape, and promote good sleeping habits. All these things help lower anxiety and stimulate the release of feel-good hormones whilst building their immunity and stamina.

7. Listen to them when they come to you. Again, giving them positive attention is one of the most important things. It is very difficult for teens to open up about their problems with a parent or sibling. They only do so when they have run out of ideas or things have gotten out of control. Therefore, when they come to you to seek advice, listen actively. Help them with whatever support, ideas, or the positive dose of energy that they need so that it reduces some of their stress.

Chapter 6: Essential Parenting Skill – Picking Battles

There are rare things that shake a parent's confidence in the way they are raising their kids. They don't question their parenting style unless their children start to exhibit bad behavior. They examine the shortcomings and challenges they still face but there is one problem – their kids are no longer kids. They are grownups who have a mind of their own. They don't just listen to you and adhere to what you say. They question. They counter your orders with their preferences. They refuse to do the things you tell them because they no longer need to be told what to do. The communication channels are also broken and no longer flow easily. It's like treading carefully into a field full of mines. The minute you take the wrong step, things blow up.

Conflicts Can Ruin Relationships

Conflicts between parents and teenagers are a common sight. With their hormones raging, teenagers often get so heated that they start to talk back, misbehave, or ignore their parents. They fight because they want to change their relationship with their parents. They have always been in the backseat of the car and now they want to be in the driver's seat. They want to live by their own rules and make decisions that concern themselves on their own. They want to be included in important discussions about the family instead of just agreeing to things mindlessly. They want to shake their parents into this new reality where they want them to see them as a new, more intellectual, and exciting person. They act over-dramatic, make mountains out of molehills, and try to push their parents into agreeing to things they are proposing.

They also want their parents to appreciate them for who they are becoming or have become even when it isn't a positive change. These quarrels, if not handled maturely, can lead to rifts between delicate relationships. For starters, it can disrupt the peace in the household and among siblings. It can also lead to blame, shame and unraveling old grievances and past failures. It can make both the parent and the teenager feel misunderstood and hurt. It can lead to anger and abuse in rare cases where one or both the parties use physical or verbal abuse to hurt one another. Some teenagers have also left their homes and moved in with their partners or friends because they feel their parents don't see them for who they are, and they are done with all the fights and violence it leads to.

Therefore, the responsibility to handle conflicts efficiently lies on the parents, as they are supposedly the more sensible ones in the relationship. This leads us to one of the most important parenting skills in today's time, picking our battles.

What Battles Are Worth Fighting and What Aren't?

Picking our battles means we critically analyze what arguments are worth stretching and what aren't. It involves thinking and deciding whether to go into action mode or not. It also means that we choose things with a profitable reward and leave the ones that pose no return on investment. As parents, we need to choose to either go into the fight or flight mood.

There will always be some issues worth fighting over and some that aren't. Your goal is to identify the ones that are and hold your ground. As for the rest, you can choose to ignore it. To make things interesting, we have created a flight and fight list to help parents understand if they are picking up the right issues to fight over or not.

The Flight List

These are the issues that can be left and ignored because fighting over them doesn't change things or bring out any positives. You will understand it more once you view the list.

Their Appearance or Clothing

It doesn't matter – at least not in the longer run – if they wish to have a certain hairstyle, get their hair dyed, or dress according to their style. They may choose to act emo and dye their hair all black or dress like a rockstar with a leather jacket on at all times. The point is, preferences change with time. They may feel in the zone right now but these choices and preferences will eventually change. They will learn to carry themselves better when they enter the professional world. So there isn't a point in starting a conflict over it every time.

A Messy Room

Some kids can't stand a dirty room. Some don't have the time to clean their rooms. A messy room isn't something you want to deal with. They can be messy eaters and careless about how their room looks, as long as they can find something clean to wear to school. Therefore, being too aggressive about it won't do you or them any good. Let it be. They will learn to behave when they move into a place of their own and spend hours looking for something.

Eating Times and Habits

Some teenagers, especially girls, give their parents a hard time with their eating habits. They will start a new diet every other week and starve themselves. They will survive on detox cleanses that taste like vomit because they have to shed a few pounds for an upcoming event. For guys, you can find them standing by the fridge, eating anything they can find in the middle of the night and then leave the kitchen a mess. Now, we do believe that healthy eating habits must be encouraged, but there are ways to go about it.

The Fight List

This list has the things you have to fight about if you see them not adhering to them. For example:

Paying Respect to Others

If they don't show others the respect that they deserve, they need to be confronted about it. It is never okay for them to be disrespectful towards their peers, parents, or teachers. They must not show prejudice toward someone or think of themselves as privileged in any way.

Curfews

They must, at all times, adhere to the rules and limitations set by you. Of course, there can be exceptions such as a class that ended late, a flat tire, or an urgent problem with a peer. They must still know to inform you about it.

Their Grades

There is no going around it. If their grades are poor, the reasons need to be discussed in a calm yet stern manner. You can scold them for not completing their homework on time or not spending time preparing for their exams.

Skills You Need to Pick Your Battles Wisely

How can you pick your battles wisely and without creating a scene every time with your teenager? Below are some great skills to use to make the right choice.

Understand the Reasons for Arguments

The first thing you need to know is why you are fighting about something. Teenagers have different personalities and styles. Some teenagers just fight for the sake of arguing. Some are shy and avoid confrontation. Some know the right things to say to change your mind and make you listen. Thus, knowing the reason for an argument combined with the personality of your child will help you pick the right battle worth fighting about.

What Are You Trying to Achieve

What is it that you wish to achieve with the conflict? What is the outcome you want? Do you just want to prove them wrong and yourself right? If so, it isn't worth the fight. Or do they want to handle waywardness and leave a positive impact on their wellbeing if they choose to change? If so, it is a worthy cause.

Getting the Timing Right

Sometimes, we are fighting the right cause but choose an inappropriate time. Kids, when in a bad mood, won't listen to you, no matter how meaningful and rewarding the outcome could be. Therefore, if you want them to listen and obey, choose the right time to have an argument or discussion.

Can a Compromise Be Made?

Is it possible that the conflict ends on a positive note where both of you settle on the same thing? Demands can be negotiated and knowing how to negotiate can reduce the pressure on you. You want them to respect you and obey you. They want the same respect in return. So try to find a middle ground where both of you leave with something, no matter how little.

Chapter 7: Essential Parenting Skill - Setting Reasonable Expectations

Think about this for a minute. Would you go to the meat shop to buy shoes? Sounds silly, correct? But many of us do this. Not this exactly, but we set the wrong expectations for others. Remember the quote about the fish being judged on her ability to climb a tree? It's senseless. So how can we judge our teenagers over the capabilities or talents they don't have?

If your teenager had the worst experience playing volleyball with her team twice, where once, she came back with a bloody nose and told you she doesn't want to play anymore, would you still push her? If so, then maybe you do look for shoes in a meat shop.

A lot of times, parents become overexcited while setting expectations for their children. If they showed a slight interest in one skill, they want them to become a pro at it. However, setting unrealistic expectations can be damaging to their self-esteem because every time they fail or disappoint you, they lose a little part of themselves out of shame and guilt. They start to lose all confidence in their abilities and see themselves as a failure. This lack of interest can land them in dark places where they seek release from all the frustration they feel about themselves.

So in this chapter, we seek answers on how parents can set realistic expectations for their children, without burdening them with too much. We shall also see the impact of setting high, low, and reasonable expectations in the second half of the chapter.

But first, what questions should you ask yourself when setting realistic expectations for your teenager?

Questions to Ask Yourself

You must know the difference between setting and having expectations. Setting expectations is a more logical and realistic approach, where you look at your child's capabilities and then set a reasonable goal for them to achieve. Having expectations is more of a wish, where you set unrealistic expectations and pray that your child lives up to them. To clarify it further, ask yourself if you are setting the right expectations or demanding them.

The first thing you need to ask is how you can know if the expectation is realistic or not. Do you think your child possesses the expertise and strength to live up to it or assume that they will develop expertise once they start trying?

Is the expectation based on something you want and something that your child wants? Again, you have to remain focused on the things they want. True, you are a better judge of what is best for them but setting unrealistic expectations won't get you the thing you want. It will only make your child feel incompetent. Maybe what you want from them is something you had wanted when you were a little child. But is it what your child wants too?

The third question to ask yourself is about the influences that push you. Are your actions and demands directed towards the betterment of your child or are you following a tradition your family had?

The Effects of High, Low and Just Right Expectations For Teenagers

Parental expectations, if set realistically, can help foster a child's self-esteem and nurture healthy development. However, this relies on the fact that expectations are set just right – meaning they aren't too high or ridiculously low. As a parent, your goal is to find a balance between the two, and hope for an outcome that doesn't affect your child negatively.

When expectations are set too high, they become unattainable for teenagers. They feel they have to be perfect and when they fail, they feel powerless and incompetent. Repeated failures can result in a lack of interest where the child either gives up too easily without trying or prevents attempting it all together.

On the other hand, when expectations are set too low, teenagers may feel a lack of direction and purpose in life. When parents don't set goals that push them into the unknown a little, they feel unmotivated. They feel like they aren't good enough to accomplish anything and thus, the low expectations from their parents. They need to have a goal and purpose in life.

Lastly, when the expectations set are just right i.e. they aren't too high or low, it helps the teenager develop a healthy sense of self-worth and competence. Realistic expectations allow children to do well and encourages them to keep moving forward without putting a lot of pressure on themselves.

Setting Realistic Expectations – the Basics

Choosing the right expectations for your teen shouldn't feel challenging. You just need to get a few basics right and hopefully, you will have a teen that excels at everything they put their mind to. Therefore, take a look at how you can set the right expectations from an early age to minimize behavioral issues in the future.

Different Children, Different Expectations

Just because your older child was good at sports doesn't mean your other one will excel in it too. Every child is different and has their own set of talents and skills. Therefore, when setting expectations, try not to burden your children with something they don't have the skills or interest for. This can frustrate them and they may feel that you have been unfair to them.

One Responsibility at a Time

Children want to make their parents proud, and the best way to feel that pride is when they live up to the expectations that parents have for them. However, if we put too much pressure or burdens on them at once, they might lose their confidence and not be able to give their best shot. Thus, let them take on one task at a time to learn about responsibility before handing them a list of what is expected of them. The more reasonable and few expectations there are at the start, the better. It will build their self-esteem and boost their confidence in themselves.

Begin Small and Then Grow

You can't expect your teenager to pick up on all the skills they need to achieve something set by you in a day. You need to give them time as well as the resources or directions when you expect something from them. Habits take time to develop and if something seems too hard the first time, there are fewer chances that your child will show interest in it later. Therefore, let them have a few wins and feel confident in themselves before setting up the bigger ones. Let them have the taste of independence and self-reliance a little, and then help them take on the bigger expectations driven by that motivation after winning.

Give It to Them in Writing

Finally, sometimes, the directives we give them are forgotten as the moment passes. For instance, maybe you were stuck in traffic with your teenager and decided it was the right time to instill some good expectations. The expectations may seem clear but can be misunderstood by them as a lecture. Therefore, if you are expecting them to do something or setting a goal for them, you have to make sure they know that it is one. The best way to do so is to put it in writing so it can't be forgotten or ignored.

Chapter 8: Essential Parenting Skill – Make Communication Stronger

As children grow, the changes in the way we communicate reflect the type of relationship we have with them. They are seeking more independence and exploring new things –things that aren't always the kind you would support. Therefore, communication may take a toll and become obsolete. But it doesn't have to. Effective communication should be the goal *always*. It doesn't matter how small or big they are, you have to keep the channels of communication open and welcoming. Effective communication happens when we allow ourselves the exposure to not just verbal words but also non-verbal gestures. We don't only hear but listen. If done properly, it can help your teenager feel more relaxed around you and have a stronger and deeper bond with you, where they don't need to hide things from you anymore. You can have even the most difficult of conversations over the dinner table without feeling awkward about it.

You must keep in mind that any communication becomes effective only when:

- Both parties feel free to talk about their feelings, be heard, and understood.
- You have the opportunity to share things without being judged.

Communicating with teens is always a challenge because of the changing dynamics in the household too. Previously, they were more dependent on you for everything, had more free time on their hands to be able to sit down and watch TV with you, but not anymore. Thus, it gets harder to know what is going on in their lives and be able to help them reduce some of the anxiety they feel.

The Goal of Effective Communication

Somewhere along the line, we all believe that effective communication happens when we understand each other's words, right? Wrong. It happens when we understand the feelings and emotions underlying their words. For instance, if your teenager comes up to you and suggests something like, "Can I skip school tomorrow? I hate going on school trips, there is so much drama." What do you think would be a great answer to that?

1. Are you saying you want to skip school because of the drama?
2. Do you feel bothered by the drama on the school trip or is there something more to it that you are not telling me?

The first one misses the point completely, as you just parroted back their words to them. The second one, however, focuses more on their feelings and ideas about the school trip, where, chances are, she feels ignored or bullied, or just anxious.

When teenagers feel that they are listened to emotionally, they feel cared for. The goal of any effective communication that happens between the two of you is this. You don't have to cut to the chase, offer them the solution to a problem they are facing right away, and get done with it. You have to do more than that. You have to understand and validate their feelings.

How Effective Communication Can Cultivate Healthy Relationships With Teenagers

So how do we help our teenagers by making communication more intimate and effective? For starters, you have to deliver clear and consistent messages. You have to give them your complete attention when they come to you to talk about something. You have to let them know, both with your words and actions, that you won't judge them, mock them, or shame them. This means your messages or words should be a pure reflection of what you think about the problem. You can't say anything else and let your body tell a different story. Other than that, here are a few tips to remember:

Be an Approachable Adult

This means your teen shouldn't have to think twice before coming up to you. They should know with certainty that you wouldn't judge them. They should know that their problems will be resolved and there will be no overreaction or shaming involved.

Provide Them With Opportunities

Sometimes, the reason teenagers avoid talking to their parents is that they always find them busy with something. Communication can't happen like this. Both partners have to be clear headed, and know that something important is being discussed. Go on a short trip together or ask them to help you do something together. Maybe that will help them open up to you.

Be Supportive

If they come to you with something, don't criticize. Anyone can make a mistake. Their mistakes may seem rather naive and deliberate but don't act too worried or stressed. Instead, help them figure out ways to make amends. Criticism will only make them feel worse about themselves and hurt their self-esteem.

Prevent Power Struggles

Power struggles happen when one or both individuals want to be proven right. Your teen may hold a strong opinion and so do you. Don't belittle the whole conversation about who is right and who isn't. This will only end with hurt feelings on both ends and, may very well, become the reason for an argument. If that happens, your child won't come up to you the next time.

Focus on Interests

If you are trying hard to talk about something with them, focus on the things that interest them to spark conversations. Sometimes, when we talk about the things we love, we get so comfortable in our conversations. That should be the goal here too. You aren't trying to make a point or lecture them about something, you just talk about stuff that interests them and hope that they respond to it.

Validate Their Feelings

As parents, it is quite natural for us to want to fix and resolve the problems our children face. Your intent might be the same. However, sometimes, they just want to feel validated and heard. They want to know that you understand what they are going through. Nothing more, just that!

Don't Accuse or Assume

Let them tell you what happened. Even if you know the truth or think that you know what happened, let them have the chance to get it off their chest before you start to accuse or assume things. Don't probe leading questions in between to disrupt the flow. Let them tell you what bothers them and then ask them if they just wanted to vent or if needed any help with it.

Chapter 9: Essential Parenting Skill - Giving Them Some Room to Breathe

The need for privacy is another developmental milestone for children. It is a natural request that teenagers make as a part of growing up. As they start to face challenges, search for their place in the world and go through many physical changes, they may act shy or wary of things concerning them.

For many parents, this is rather challenging. For years, they have been the only provider of their needs, and all of a sudden, they want them out. It can be both hurtful and difficult to adjust that they are no longer a priority in the lives of their children. But just because they want to have the door of their room closed at all times, tell you not to look in their school bag or befriend them on social media accounts doesn't mean they are hiding something from you. It can simply mean that they feel protective about their choices and the information about themselves. It can only be considered a red flag if they have started to depict some behavioral changes and acting a little weird.

The Need for Privacy in a Teenager's Life

Teens don't only need independence as they grow, they also want to be trusted to do things by themselves. They want to be seen as mature, and trustworthy adults who can take responsibility for things and handle their problems. Giving your teenagers some privacy and space can allow them to develop into inspiring adults. The level of trust you have in them makes them feel confident and capable.

Teens, when they endure physical changes become cautious about themselves. The child who once felt comfortable bathing naked in the pool on a sunny day doesn't feel that way anymore. They will lock their door before disrobing. They will also close the door when talking to their partner or friends about a party or an event where they are expected to show up.

Privacy, when allowed in the right measure can help with fostering the bond with the teen and their parents. They may start to ask for your advice with some personal problems if they think you will show respect in return, and not be too judgmental. They may also seek guidance from you about their plans.

Setting Rules for Privacy – A Beginner's Guide for Parents

Teenagers need space and privacy to do things their way. Therefore, doing things like going through their diary or journal, or checking the pockets of their jeans or school bag without their permission is a big no-no. Unless of course, your concerns are for their safety and they have been acting shady for a few days or weeks. Boundaries allow them to learn about responsibility. Besides, it is highly unethical to go through their stuff without their knowledge because it can damage the trust between the two of you. Imagine, if someone searched your drawers without your permission. Would you not see it as a breach of your privacy?

Since the goal is to improve the relationship between the parent and the teenager, you have to act sensibly and make them feel safe in their house. Some healthy ways to set boundaries and rules for privacy should look like this:

Seek Input

If you are going to set some ground rules for them, the least you can do is include them too. Have a debate over curfew times and how much screen time should be allowed and reach a mutual decision. This will make them feel validated and not make you a strict parent.

Have Important Discussions Frequently

Keep in mind, the term frequently doesn't mean all the time here. Talking to your teens about stuff like drugs, sex, addictions, and bullying from time to time can keep the door open for communication. Don't be too outspoken and inquisitive. Try to blend it into normal conversations to seek their opinions about it.

Watch Out for Them

Keep an eye on their school performance, relationships, and social media without trying to micromanage. Knowing what is going on in their lives can help you understand them better.

Put Limits on Digital Media

From the very beginning, let them know beforehand that you will be asking them about the apps installed on their phones regularly. You can also have them install tracking and monitoring apps on their phones, not to spy, but to always know that they are safe. They should know of your intentions too, so that they don't think you don't trust them.

Knock Before Entering

If you know they are in the room and the room isn't locked, it is still wise to knock before entering without an announcement. That would be an invasion of their privacy and they will make sure to have it locked the next time, even when they weren't doing something suspicious. Therefore, don't let your hastiness take away the trust they have in you.

Leave the Room When at the Doctor's

It is humiliating to have to declare in front of your parents that you have been active sexually when they don't even know that you have a partner. This is why a doctor's visit can be rather unpleasant and shocking. If, as their parent, you sense the uneasiness on their face when asked intimate questions about their sexuality, excuse yourself to leave the room to let them be open with their doctor in peace. They will come to you when they feel confident enough to share something as intimate as this with you.

Conclusion

Teenagers aren't a different breed as we often think. Everyone is quick to judge them for being rebellious, ill-disciplined, and rude. But this isn't the case with all teenagers. Some are just an extension of their former self with a few upgrades. They are still closely connected to their parents, have strong bonds with their friends, respect their peers, and are known to be the most empathetic people in their class and among peers.

The hero is, of course, the parent/parents who instill the right values and morals from the start. They use effective parenting skills to nurture, discipline, and instill responsibility to raise successful and competent kids. They value honesty, trust, and happiness because these seem to be the ethics people care about in the professional world. They teach them to have manners, show empathy and be compassionate towards others which makes them a great and kind individual.

Your job is to impart the same wisdom in them to help them prepare themselves for the next phase of their lives. If you think that they are too old to be taught something new, you are wrong. You can always preach about something if you do it the right way. You just have to be strategic about it in a way that it doesn't come off as a lecture or a demand but rather, a suggestion. You have to let them choose or at least let them have a say.

If we quickly review the book, we notice we have done almost the same. We have put into practice various parenting skills, but left it on them, the teenager, to decide if they want to follow those rules or not. We used different strategic ways to impart that knowledge, such as becoming the prime example, allowing them some space to themselves, lending our time and ears to them to make communication more effective, picking the fights worth fighting and ignoring the ones that aren't, setting reasonable expectations, and helping them find ways to reduce anxiety and depression.

Hopefully, this book will leave you with many new and implementable ways to deal with teen anxiety, foster strong relationships with them, and make communication smoother and easier. If you liked the advice and found it useful, someone else will too. Let us know what you think of it and how you found it helpful.

Thank you for giving this book a read. I hope you loved reading it as much as I enjoyed writing it. It would make me the happiest person on earth if you would take a moment to leave an honest review. All you have to do is visit the site where you purchased this book: It's that simple! The review doesn't have to be a full-fledged paragraph; a few words will do. Your few words will help others decide if this is what they should be reading as well. Thank you in advance, and best of luck with your parenting adventures. Every moment is a joyous one with a child.

References

Anxiety in teenagers. (2019, February). Raising
  Children Network.
  https://raisingchildren.net.au/pre-
  teens/mental-health-physical-health/stress-
  anxiety-depression/anxiety

Any Anxiety Disorder. (2017, November). Nih.Gov.
  https://www.nimh.nih.gov/health/statistics/
  any-anxiety-disorder.shtml#part_155096

Coleman, P. K. (2003). Perceptions of parent-child
  attachment, social self-efficacy, and peer
  relationships in middle childhood. Infant and
  Child Development, 12(4), 351–368.
  https://doi.org/10.1002/icd.316

Damico, P. (2017, November 28). 7 Common Causes
  of Teenage Anxiety. Paradigm Malibu.
  https://paradigmmalibu.com/common-
  causes-teenage-anxiety/

Duineveld, J. J., Parker, P. D., Ryan, R. M.,
  Ciarrochi, J., & Salmela-Aro, K. (2017). The
  link between perceived maternal and paternal
  autonomy support and adolescent well-being
  across three major educational transitions.
  Developmental Psychology, 53(10), 1978–
  1994. https://doi.org/10.1037/dev0000364

Eagan, K., Stolzenberg, E. B., Ramirez, J. J., Aragon, M. C., Suchard, M., & Rios-Aguilar, C. (2016). The American Freshman: Fifty-Year Trends 1966–2015 (pp. 1–352). Higher Education Research Institute.

Hall, M. (2013, May 29). How to Set Realistic Expectations for your Teenager. GoNannies.Com. https://www.gonannies.com/blog/2013/how-to-set-realistic-expectations-for-your-teenager/

Joussemet, M., Landry, R., & Koestner, R. (2008). A self-determination theory perspective on parenting. Canadian Psychology/Psychologie Canadienne, 49(3), 194–200. https://doi.org/10.1037/a0012754

Martinelli, K. (n.d.). The Power of Positive Attention. Child Mind Institute. Retrieved June 3, 2020, from https://childmind.org/article/the-power-of-positive-attention/

McCarthy, C. (2019, November 20). Anxiety in Teens is Rising: What's Going On? HealthyChildren.Org. https://www.healthychildren.org/English/health-issues/conditions/emotional-problems/Pages/Anxiety-Disorders.aspx

Morin, A. (2017, August 17). The 1 Skill College Students Wish Their Parents Had Taught Them. Psychology Today. https://www.psychologytoday.com/intl/blog/what-mentally-strong-people-dont-do/201708/the-1-skill-college-students-wish-their-parents

Morin, A. (2019, September 23). This Might Be the Simplest But Most Effective Way to Prevent Behavior Problems. Verywell Family. https://www.verywellfamily.com/positive-attention-reduces-behavioral-problems-1094784

Murray, T. A. (2018, March 30). Picking your battles: the core of parenting a teen. Thrive Global. https://thriveglobal.com/stories/picking-your-battles-the-core-of-parenting/

Paxson, M. S. (2017). Setting Realistic Expectations. CHADD. https://chadd.org/attention-article/setting-realistic-expectations/

Seifert, C. (2018, November 28). What Effects Do Parental Expectations Have on Kids? Hello Motherhood. https://www.hellomotherhood.com/what-effects-do-parental-expectations-have-on-kids-9634703.html

Teen Role Models: Who They Are, Why They Matter. (2011, January 31). Barna Group. https://www.barna.com/research/teen-role-models-who-they-are-why-they-matter/

Understanding Adolescence. (n.d.). Skills You Need. Retrieved June 3, 2020, from https://www.skillsyouneed.com/parent/understanding-adolescence.html

Witmer, D. (2020, March 23). Privacy and Trust Go Hand-in-Hand for Teens (A. Morin (Ed.)). Verywell Family. https://www.verywellfamily.com/why-does-my-teen-need-privacy-2609615

Youth Index 2019. (2019). In Prince's Trust (pp. 1–11). https://www.princes-trust.org.uk/about-the-trust/research-policies-reports/youth-index-2019#:~:text=Youth%20Index%202019,people%20aged%2016%20to%2025.

www.ingramcontent.com/pod-product-compliance
Lightning Source LLC
LaVergne TN
LVHW051427080426
835508LV00022B/3271